GREAT BARBECUE RECIPES

There's always a relaxed and happy atmosphere when food is sizzling away over a barbecue! And the food always seems to taste so much better when it is cooked over the coals. It's better for you, too, as barbecuing is one of the healthiest cooking methods.

This collection of recipes for the barbecue includes old favourites as well as some that may be new to you. We're sure you'll find them all interesting and absolutely delicious. Because of the increasing popularity of food cooked on skewers, we've devoted a whole chapter to brochettes, kebabs and satays, some of which are quite spicy. And there's another chapter that's full of recipes guaranteed to keep all the spice-lovers even happier!

Although barbecues are usually informal affairs for family and friends, there are often special occasions that you feel you would like to celebrate more formally on the patio or the deck. So, for those special times, we have compiled two menus where the barbecue takes centre stage. To round off your barbecued meals, look in the last chapter for those barbecue extras – more great ideas for vegetable accompaniments, salads, interesting breads and refreshing desserts.

CONTENTS

Favourite Grills

A barbecue is a wonderful way to get together with family and friends and enjoy delicious meals cooked outdoors. All your favourite cuts of meat plus sausages, chicken and fish are here, along with some exciting new ways to cook them over the barbecue. There are also recipes for cooking vegetables and, as no barbecue is complete without a salad or two, you'll also find some salad recipes in this chapter.

Steaks on the Grill

185-250g (6-8oz) steak per person such as rump, T-bone, sirloin, Scotch fillet

vegetable or olive oil

marinades or seasonings, optional, see below

For individual steaks, cut meat 2.5cm (1in) thick. If cooking meat in a single large piece, cut it 3.5-5cm (1½-2in) thick. Marinate or season (if desired) before cooking. Place meat on an oiled rack 7.5cm (3in) above moderately hot coals. Sear steaks quickly on both sides to seal in juices, then move to a cooler area of the rack and cook to doneness desired, turning once. Serve immediately.

Marinades and Seasonings

The following quantities are enough for 4 steaks or 1kg (2lb) meat.
● Wine Marinade: Combine 250ml (8fl oz) red or white wine, 1 sliced onion, 1 tspn black peppercorns, 1 bay leaf, 4 parsley sprigs, ½ tspn dried thyme and 4 tblspn oil. Marinate steak, lamb or chicken for 1 hour at room temperature or for several hours in the refrigerator.
● Mustard Steak: Beat 125g (4oz) butter with 3 tspn dry mustard and spread over steak.
● Pepper Steak: Press coarsely cracked black pepper into steak on both sides and allow to stand for 30 minutes.
● Herbed Steak: Rub steaks with olive oil, then crumbled rosemary, thyme or oregano.

Ginger Chicken

60ml (2fl oz) soy sauce

2 tblspn grated fresh ginger

1 tblspn honey

¼ tspn freshly ground black pepper

1.5kg (3lb) chicken pieces or marylands (leg and thigh joints)

1 Combine soy sauce, ginger, honey and black pepper in a shallow dish, add chicken and marinate for 1-2 hours, turning once or twice. Drain, reserving marinade.

2 Grill chicken over hot coals, turning and basting with marinade, for 20 minutes or until tender and well glazed.

Serves 4

Foil Barbecued Potatoes

Scrub medium-size baking potatoes and cook in boiling water for 20 minutes. Drain, dry well, rub with a little butter or oil and wrap each potato in aluminium foil. Cook potatoes in coals or on barbecue grill, turning occasionally, for 20 minutes or until tender when pierced with a skewer. To serve, pull back foil, cut a cross in top of each potato, squeeze open and season or fill as desired.

Foil Barbecued Potatoes, Steaks on the Grill, Ginger Chicken

Oriental Beef Ribs

Oriental Beef Ribs

1.5kg (3lb) beef spareribs, trimmed

Oriental Sauce

500ml (16fl oz) water

4 tblspn soy sauce

2 tblspn rice wine vinegar

2 tspn sesame seeds

2 tspn brown sugar

2 tspn sesame oil

2 cloves garlic, crushed

1 tspn freshly ground black pepper

1 Place spareribs in a large saucepan, cover with cold water, bring to simmering and simmer for 10 minutes. Drain well and set aside.

2 To make sauce, place water, soy sauce, vinegar, sesame seeds, sugar, sesame oil, garlic and black pepper in same pan over a medium heat and bring to the boil. Add ribs, cover and reduce heat. Gently simmer for 45 minutes or until beef is almost tender. Drain, reserving sauce.

3 Cook ribs on an oiled grill rack over hot coals, turning and basting frequently with sauce, for 20 minutes or until tender and well glazed. Serve with remaining sauce.

Serves 6

Waikiki Steak

6 Scotch fillet (rib eye) steaks, each about 2.5cm (1in) thick

1/4 stalk celery

125ml (4fl oz) soy sauce

60ml (2fl oz) peanut or vegetable oil

60ml (2fl oz) red wine

1 clove garlic, crushed

1 Place steaks in a shallow glass dish. Chop celery and press through a garlic press, or finely grate. Rub celery and celery juice into the meat. Combine soy sauce, oil, wine and garlic, pour over steaks and set aside to marinate for 30 minutes.

2 Drain steaks, reserving marinade. Cook on an oiled grill rack over hot coals, brushing occasionally with marinade, for 7 minutes on each side or until cooked to doneness desired.

Serves 6

Grilled Citrus Chicken

2 large oranges

1 small onion, sliced into thin rings

1 tblspn sherry

4-6 chicken pieces

1 tblspn vegetable oil

1 tblspn lemon juice

salt

parsley or watercress for garnish

1. Using a vegetable peeler, thinly peel rind from oranges and cut into julienne strips. Place strips and onion in a bowl, add sherry and set aside to marinate.

2. Brush chicken with oil, sprinkle with half the lemon juice and season with salt to taste. Grill, skin-side-down, over moderately hot coals, turning and brushing frequently with oil, for 15-20 minutes or until tender.

3. Peel oranges, removing all pith, and cut into thin slices. Place chicken on a heated platter. Sprinkle orange strips, onion rings and remaining lemon juice on top, surround with orange slices, and garnish with parsley or watercress.

Serves 4

Barbecued Garlic Chicken

| 2 x 1.2kg (2lb7oz) chickens, halved |
| 3 cloves garlic, crushed |
| 1 tspn salt |
| 2 tblspn lemon juice |
| 90ml (3fl oz) vegetable oil |

Garlic Sauce

| 12 cloves garlic |
| 1 tspn salt |
| 185ml (6fl oz) olive oil |
| 2 tblspn lemon juice |
| 1 tblspn boiling water |

1. Pat chicken dry with paper towels and remove wing tips. Place crushed garlic, salt, lemon juice and vegetable oil in a small bowl and beat well to combine. Rub the chicken with half the mixture and set aside to marinate for at least 2 hours.

2. Place chicken, skin-side-up, on an oiled grill rack over moderately hot coals and cook for 15 minutes. Turn and cook, basting frequently with remaining marinade, for 10 minutes longer or until tender.

3. To make sauce, place garlic, salt and 1 tablespoon olive oil in a blender or food processor and process to make a smooth paste. With machine running, slowly add remaining oil and process until thick. Add lemon juice and water and process to combine. Serve sauce with chicken.

Serves 4

Grilled Citrus Chicken

Italian Grilled Chicken on Greens

Use a mixture of several different salad greens with watercress and witloof (chicory) – wash well and spin dry, then chill in a plastic food bag until crisp.

4 tblspn lemon juice
1/2 onion, finely chopped
1-2 tblspn olive oil
1-2 cloves garlic, optional
1 tspn dried oregano
salt
freshly ground black pepper
2 small chickens, quartered
assorted salad greens

1 Combine lemon juice, onion, oil, garlic (if using), oregano, salt and black pepper to taste in a large shallow glass dish. Add chicken, turning to coat, and set aside to marinate for at least 1 hour.

2 Drain chicken, reserving marinade. Place, skin-side-down, on an oiled grill rack over moderately hot coals and cook for 5 minutes. Turn, baste with marinade, and cook for 10 minutes more. Turn and cook for 5 minutes longer or until chicken is tender and juices run clear when pierced. Serve on a bed of mixed greens.

Serves 4

Grilled Tarragon Chicken

6 chicken breast fillets
1 clove garlic
salt
2 tspn dried tarragon
30g (1oz) butter, softened, or 2 tblspn olive oil
balsamic or sherry vinegar

1 Wipe chicken breasts dry with paper towels. Crush garlic with a little salt in a small bowl, add tarragon, butter or oil and vinegar and mix to make a smooth paste. Spread over both sides of breasts, pushing a little between flesh and skin. Set aside to stand for several hours.

2 Grill chicken, skin-side-down, over moderately hot coals for 5-10 minutes, then turn and cook 10-15 minutes more, turning once or twice, or until chicken is tender and skin crisp and golden.

Serves 6

Melon and Berries

1 small rockmelon (cantaloupe), quartered
315g (10oz) strawberries, halved
100g (3 1/2 oz) blueberries
2 tblspn icing sugar
2 tblspn white rum or orange-flavoured liqueur, optional

Slice the flesh off melon wedges, cube the flesh and replace in melon shells. Place berries in a bowl, add icing sugar and rum or liqueur (if using) and gently toss to coat. Spoon berries over melon wedges and serve.

Serves 4

Italian Grilled Chicken on Greens, Melon and Berries

Chicken, Corn Pancakes and Chilli Butter

Quick and light, grilled chicken is one of the best summer dishes. Pancakes and a zesty butter are delicious and unusual ways to dress up the bird when guests stay for dinner.

4 tblspn lemon juice

3 tblspn olive oil

2-3 fresh thyme sprigs or 1 tspn dried thyme

1/4 tspn ground sweet paprika

salt

freshly ground black pepper

6 chicken breast fillets

Corn Pancakes

315g (10oz) sweet corn kernels cut straight from the cobs or frozen corn, defrosted

125ml (4fl oz) double cream

1 egg

45g (1 1/2oz) plain flour

1/2 tspn salt

1/4 tspn sugar

30g (1oz) butter, melted

extra butter for frying

Chilli Butter

60g (2oz) butter, softened

1 tblspn tomato purée

2 tspn finely grated orange rind

few drops Tabasco sauce

freshly ground black pepper

1 To make Chilli Butter, place butter, tomato purée, orange rind, Tabasco and black pepper to taste in a bowl and mix well to combine. Place mixture on a piece of aluminium foil or plastic food wrap and gently roll to shape into a log. Refrigerate until firm.

2 Place lemon juice, oil, thyme, paprika and salt and black pepper to taste in a large shallow dish and mix to combine. Add chicken breasts, turning to coat, cover and set aside to marinate at room temperature for 1-2 hours, or in the refrigerator overnight.

3 To make pancakes, place corn kernels, cream, egg, flour, salt, sugar and melted butter in a blender or food processor and process until mixture is smooth. Place a large, heavy frying pan over a medium-high heat and, when hot, brush lightly with extra butter. Drop mixture, 2 tablespoons at a time, into pan and fry pancakes, turning once, until cooked and golden on both sides. Place on a heated plate, cover loosely and set aside to keep warm.

4 Drain chicken, reserving marinade. Place, skin-side-down, over moderately hot coals and cook for 5 minutes. Turn and cook, basting occasionally with marinade, for 3-5 minutes longer or until tender and juices run clear when pierced with a skewer.

5 To serve, arrange chicken on a serving dish with the pancakes. Cut seasoned butter crosswise into rounds, place a round on each chicken breast and serve immediately.

Serves 6

Best Barbecued Sausages

An enticingly wide range of sausages is available in packages or loose from butchers, food stores and delicatessens. They may be thick, thin or chipolata (cocktail sausages). Sausages require careful cooking so the outside is crispy brown and the centre cooked through, but not dry. Blanching the sausages first plumps up the meal or filler, releases some of the fat and ensures that thick sausages will be cooked through. Separate sausages by cutting between the links with a sharp knife. Place in a saucepan, cover with cold water,

bring to the boil and simmer gently for 5 minutes. Drain, then pierce sausages all over with a skewer. Place sausages, in 1 layer, on an oiled rack over moderately hot coals and cook, turning constantly, for 10-15 minutes for thick sausages, 5-8 minutes for thin ones, or until cooked through and browned.

Orange Glazed Pork Sausages

600g (1lb 2oz) pork sausages or chipolatas

Orange Marinade

60ml (2fl oz) orange juice concentrate

60ml (2fl oz) tomato sauce

2 cloves garlic, crushed

1 onion, grated

1 tblspn olive oil

2 tblspn lemon juice

2 tblspn honey

1 Place sausages in a large saucepan, cover with cold water, bring to simmering over a medium heat and simmer for 5 minutes. Drain and pierce well.

2 To make marinade, place juice concentrate, tomato sauce, garlic, onion, oil, lemon juice and honey in a shallow dish and mix to combine. Add sausages, turning to coat, cover and set aside to marinate, turning occasionally, for 2 hours at room temperature.

3 Drain sausages, reserving marinade. Place on an oiled grill rack over moderately hot coals and cook, turning and brushing frequently with marinade, for 5-10 minutes or until cooked through and well glazed.

Serves 4

Chicken, Corn Pancakes and Chilli Butter

Trout with Green and Gold Sauce

How do you serve a crowd without slaving over the fire when you'd rather be looking after your guests? Barbecue whole fish at your leisure before the guests arrive, spoon this fragrant sauce over while the fish is hot and serve it just warm or cold – as it cools, the fish will absorb the sauce deliciously.

2 x 750g (1¹/₂lb) whole trout, scaled and cleaned

1 lemon, thinly sliced

2 sage or bay leaves

1 small onion, sliced

salt

freshly ground black pepper

olive oil or melted butter

fresh herbs or watercress for garnish

Green and Gold Sauce

3 large lemons

90ml (3fl oz) red wine vinegar

1 tspn Dijon mustard

170ml (5¹/₂fl oz) olive oil

4 tblspn finely chopped fresh parsley

4 tblspn chopped fresh tarragon or basil or 2 tspn dried tarragon or basil

1-2 cloves garlic, crushed

1 To make sauce, peel lemons, removing all pith, and cut into thin slices, removing any seeds. Place vinegar and mustard in a bowl and gradually whisk in oil, a little at a time, until thickened and combined. Add lemon slices, parsley, tarragon or basil and garlic and season to taste with salt and black pepper.

2 Rinse trout and pat dry on paper towels. Fill cavities of fish with unpeeled lemon slices, sage or bay leaves and onion. Season to taste with salt and black pepper and brush skin with oil or butter.

3 Cover the grill bars or hotplate of a barbecue with greased aluminium foil. Place fish on foil over moderately hot coals and cook for 5 minutes. Turn fish and cook 10-15 minutes longer, or until flesh flakes easily.

4 Remove from heat. When cool enough to handle, carefully peel off skin from one side of each fish, leaving head and tail intact. Place on serving platter, garnish with herbs or watercress and spoon sauce over fish. Serve hot or at room temperature.

Serves 6

Grilled Squid (Calamari)

You can use the flat hotplate of the barbecue or a cast iron frying pan over the grill rack. Choose small squid (calamari) for this quick cooking method and serve as soon as they turn opaque, as the flesh seems to toughen on standing. If fresh squid (calamari) is unavailable, substitute with defrosted frozen rings.

500g (1lb) small cleaned squid (calamari)

125ml (4fl oz) olive oil

¹/₂ tspn ground paprika

few drops Tabasco sauce

salt

freshly ground pepper

chopped fresh parsley

2 lemons, quartered

1 Clean squid (calamari), pulling out tentacles and beak, wash and pat dry on paper towels. Leave whole if very small, or cut lengthwise into 2 or 4 pieces – or into fine strips or rings and place in a bowl. Add oil, paprika, Tabasco sauce and mix well. Season to taste with salt and black pepper. Set aside to marinate, stirring occasionally, for 2 hours.

2 Grill the squid (calamari) with the marinade on a barbecue hotplate over hot coals, turning often, for 3-4 minutes or until opaque, taking care not to overcook. Sprinkle with parsley and serve immediately garnished with lemon quarters.

Serves 4

Barbecued Tuna

750g (1¹/₂lb) fresh tuna

60ml (2fl oz) vegetable oil

2 tblspn white vinegar

salt

4 fresh thyme sprigs

3 tblspn chopped fresh parsley

1 Trim any dark flesh from tuna and cut into 4 steaks. Place oil, vinegar and salt to taste in a shallow glass dish and mix to combine. Add tuna steaks, turning to coat, and set aside to marinate for 1 hour.

2 Drain tuna, reserving marinade. Place steaks in a fish grill or on the hotplate of the barbecue with the thyme sprigs over moderately hot coals. Cook, basting with marinade, for 3-5 minutes on each side or until golden and flesh flakes easily. Serve sprinkled with parsley.

Serves 4

Golden Grilled Fish Steaks

4 x 155g (5oz) firm fish steaks or thick fillets

15g (¹/₂oz) butter, melted

2 tomatoes, peeled, seeded and diced

4 tblspn mayonnaise (preferably homemade)

salt

freshly ground black pepper

Brush fish with melted butter and place on an oiled barbecue hotplate over hot coals (skin-side-down for fillets). Cook for 3-4 minutes. Turn fish over, top with tomatoes and mayonnaise and cook for 3-4 minutes longer, or until golden brown and flesh flakes easily. Season to taste with salt and black pepper and serve.

Serves 4

Barbecued Lemon Sardines

Look for small sardines about 10cm (4in) long and cook them whole. If using larger fish, remove the heads, slit the stomach and remove entrails before cooking.

24 fresh sardines, cleaned

salt

freshly ground black pepper

3 tblspn lemon juice

60ml (2fl oz) vegetable or olive oil

60g (2oz) breadcrumbs, made from stale bread

chopped fresh parsley for garnish

3 lemons, quartered to serve

1 Place sardines in a bowl with salt and black pepper to taste. Add lemon juice and oil and lightly mix to coat. Set aside to marinate for 30 minutes.

2 Drain and roll sardines in breadcrumbs, pressing firmly to coat. Place on a piece of greased aluminium foil on the grill rack or hotplate over hot coals and cook for 2-3 minutes on each side, or until cooked through and golden. Sprinkle with parsley and serve immediately with lemon quarters.

Serves 4

Lemon Ginger Chops

4 tblspn vegetable oil

1 tspn grated fresh ginger

1 tspn grated lemon rind

1 tblspn lemon juice

1 tblspn brown sugar

salt

freshly ground black pepper

4 large lamb shoulder or leg chops

1 Place oil, ginger, lemon rind, lemon juice, sugar, salt and black pepper to taste in a shallow glass dish and mix well to combine. Add chops, turning to coat, cover and set aside in the refrigerator to marinate at least several hours or overnight.

2 Drain chops, reserving marinade. Grill over hot coals, turning and basting with marinade, for 10-15 minutes or until tender.

Serves 4

Grilled Cutlets and Vegetables

8 lamb cutlets, well trimmed

2 tomatoes, halved

4 large flat mushrooms

8 baby squash or zucchini (courgettes), halved or thickly sliced

Lemon Marinade

4 tblspn chopped mixed fresh herbs such as parsley, thyme, mint, oregano

4 tblspn olive oil

1 tblspn lemon juice

1 clove garlic, chopped

freshly ground black pepper

1 To make marinade, place herbs, oil, lemon juice, garlic and black pepper to taste in a bowl and mix to combine. Brush cutlets and vegetables with marinade, place in a ceramic dish. Add remaining marinade, cover and referigerate for 1 hour, turning once or twice.

2 Arrange cutlets on grill rack and vegetables on the hotplate over moderately hot coals and cook for 3 minutes. Turn, brush with marinade and grill for 3-4 minutes longer or until lamb is tender.

Serves 4

Grilled Lamb Steaks

For the best looking steaks, ask the butcher to cut them from the leg where the bone is thin.

125ml (4fl oz) olive oil

90ml (3fl oz) lemon juice

4 tblspn chopped mixed fresh rosemary, marjoram, parsley and chives

salt

freshly ground black pepper

4 x 155g (5oz) lamb leg steaks or chops

1 lemon, quartered for garnish

1 Place oil, lemon juice, herbs, salt and black pepper to taste in a small shallow dish and mix to combine. Add lamb, turning to coat, cover and marinate in the referigerator for several hours or overnight.

2 Drain and cook lamb on a lightly oiled hotplate or grill rack over hot coals for 5 minutes on each side or until cooked to doneness desired. Garnish with lemon and serve with a tomato-onion salad and steamed minted beans.

Serves 4

Pork Chops with Basil Butter

1-2 tblspn olive oil

6 pork chops

Basil Butter

60g (2oz) unsalted butter

1 tspn grated lemon rind

1 tspn lemon juice

1 tblspn finely chopped spring onions

2 tblspn chopped fresh basil leaves

salt

freshly ground black pepper

1 To make butter, beat butter in a small bowl until creamy, adding lemon rind, then lemon juice, spring onions, basil, salt and black pepper to taste. Shape mixture into a roll and wrap in a piece of aluminium foil. Chill until firm, for at least 1 hour.

2 Pat chops dry with paper towels and season with black pepper to taste. Cook on an oiled grill rack over moderately hot coals for 5-8 minutes on each side or until golden and tender. Top each chop with one or two thin slices Basil Butter and serve immediately.

Serves 6

Grilled Lamb Steaks

Tropical Pork and Fruit

4 pork loin chops or butterfly steaks

salt

freshly ground black pepper

1 tblspn fresh rosemary leaves or
1/2 teaspoon dried rosemary

1 tblspn vegetable or olive oil

4 fresh or canned pineapple rings

4 bananas

1 Slash pork skin and fat at intervals to stop curling, or trim fat right off, if preferred. Sprinkle chops lightly with salt, black pepper and rosemary and brush with oil.

2 Cook on an oiled grill rack over moderately hot coals for 6-8 minutes, turning several times and brushing with oil. Brush pineapple rings with oil, place on the grill with bananas still in their skins and cook for 6-8 minutes longer or until pork is tender and pineapple is golden on both sides.

3 Serve chops with pineapple rings and bananas, peeled, or with just a strip of skin taken from each.

Serves 4

Mixed Grilled Vegetables

1 eggplant (aubergine), thickly sliced lengthwise

2 onions, thickly sliced

2 large tomatoes, halved

3-4 zucchini (courgettes), sliced lengthwise

185g (6oz) flat mushrooms

Seasoned Oil

60ml (2fl oz) olive or vegetable oil

2 cloves garlic, crushed

1 tblspn finely chopped onion

1/2 tspn salt

1 fresh red chilli, chopped, optional

1 To make oil, place oil, garlic, onion, salt and red chilli (if using) in a screwtop jar and shake well to combine. Set aside to stand for several hours to allow flavours to develop.

2 Place vegetables on an oiled rack over moderately hot coals, brush well with oil mixture and cook for 5 minutes. Turn vegetables, baste again and cook 2-3 minutes longer or until tender. Serve immediately with grilled meats.

Serves 4

Pork Chops with Mango

4 pork loin chops

salt

freshly ground black pepper

1 tblspn vegetable oil

2 cloves garlic, crushed

1 tblspn Worcestershire sauce

1/2 tspn dry mustard

60g (2oz) butter

440g (14oz) canned mango slices, drained, or 1 fresh mango, stoned, peeled and sliced

1 Use a sharp knife to cut through fat around chops at 2cm (3/4in) intervals. Season to taste with salt and black pepper. Place oil, garlic, Worcestershire sauce and mustard in a screwtop jar and shake well to combine. Brush oil mixture over chops on both sides. Melt half the butter.

2 Place chops on an oiled grill rack over moderately hot coals and cook, brushing with butter every 2 minutes, for 6 minutes or until cooked through and tender.

3 Fry mango slices gently in remaining butter on a barbecue hotplate or in a frying pan. Scatter mango slices over chops and serve immediately.

Serves 4

Pork with Lemon and Sage

4 pork loin chops

olive oil

8-12 fresh sage leaves

freshly ground black pepper

60ml (2fl oz) lemon juice

salt

lemon wedges for garnish

1 Brush chops with oil, top each with 2-3 sage leaves and season well with black pepper. Sprinkle chops with lemon juice and set aside to marinate for 1 hour.

2 Place chops on an oiled grill rack over moderately hot coals and cook for 5 minutes or until golden. Turn chops, brush again with oil, and cook for 5 minutes longer or until tender.

2 Arrange chops on a heated serving platter, season to taste with salt and garnish with lemon wedges.

Serves 4

Tropical Pork and Fruit, Mixed Grilled Vegetables

SKEWER SPECIALS

Food cooked on a skewer has enormous appeal, especially for busy people, as it can be so quick and economical for everyday meals. Skewers also dress up so beautifully for entertaining that it's no wonder they are seen at all the best barbecues these days. The marinades and seasonings used in preparation are often the secret to the unique and delicious flavours achieved when skewered foods are barbecued.

Moroccan Brochettes

1.5kg (3lb) boned lamb, cut from the leg, shoulder or chump

2 onions, quartered

2 green peppers, cut into squares

Ginger and Cumin Marinade

4 tblspn lemon juice

2 tblspn olive or vegetable oil

1 small onion, grated

1 tspn salt

1 tspn ground cumin

1 tspn grated fresh ginger

freshly ground black pepper

1 To make marinade, place lemon juice, oil, grated onion, salt, cumin, ginger and black pepper to taste in a ceramic or glass bowl and mix to combine. Trim excess fat from lamb and cut into large cubes. Add lamb to marinade, stir to coat well and set aside to marinate for at least 2 hours.

2 Separate onion quarters into petals. Thread meat onto skewers alternately with pepper squares and onion pieces, not too closely together.

3 Cook kebabs on an oiled grill rack over hot coals, turning frequently, for 8-10 minutes or until lamb is crusty brown on the outside but still pink in the centre.

Serves 8

Beef and Pork Diable

500g (1lb) boneless beef, cubed

500g (1lb) boneless pork, cubed

Mustard Fruit Marinade

1 onion, grated

1 tblspn snipped fresh chives

1 tblspn chopped fresh parsley

1 tblspn soy sauce

$1\frac{1}{2}$ tblspn French mustard

2 tblspn fruit chutney

pinch dried thyme

freshly ground black pepper

1 Cut beef and pork into 2.5cm (1in) cubes and thread alternately onto small pre-soaked wooden skewers.

2 To make marinade, place onion, chives, parsley, soy sauce, mustard, chutney, thyme and black pepper to taste in a small bowl and mix well to combine. Spread mixture over meat, cover and set aside to marinate at room temperature for at least 2 hours.

3 Place skewers on an oiled grill rack over medium coals and cook slowly, turning frequently, until tender and golden brown.

Serves 6

Moroccan Brochettes, Tabbouleh (recipe page 46)

Pork and Stuffed Pepper Kebabs

This aromatic mixture is delicious pushed off the skewer into pocket bread and topped with sliced radish or a spoonful of tomato salad.

1kg (2lb) pork fillet, cut into 4cm (1¹/₂in) cubes

12 small bay leaves

Mint and Garlic Marinade

125ml (4fl oz) olive oil

60ml (2fl oz) lemon juice

60ml (2fl oz) white or red wine

2 tblspn chopped fresh mint or coriander

3 cloves garlic, crushed

salt

freshly ground black pepper

Stuffed Pepper Rolls

2 red peppers, each cut into 6 wide strips

125g (4oz) breadcrumbs, made from stale bread

1 small onion, finely chopped

2 tblspn chopped fresh mint or coriander

¹/₂ tspn ground cumin

1 tblspn lemon juice

45-60g (1¹/₂-2oz) butter, melted

1 To make marinade, place oil, lemon juice, wine, mint or coriander and garlic in a bowl, mix well and season to taste with salt and black pepper. Add pork cubes, cover and set aside to marinate for 2 hours. Drain well, reserving marinade.

2 To make pepper rolls, blanch red pepper strips in a saucepan of simmering water for 3-5 minutes or until pliable. Drain and pat dry on paper towels. Peel skin from pepper strips and discard. Place breadcrumbs, onion, mint or coriander, cumin and salt and black pepper to taste in a bowl, add lemon juice and mix with enough melted butter to make a mixture that holds together.

3 Roll tablespoons of the mixture into pepper strips and thread 2 rolls alternately with 2 bay leaves and 3 cubes of pork onto each of the 6 metal skewers.

4 Cook on an oiled grill rack over medium coals, turning occasionally and basting with marinade, for 20-25 minutes, or until pork is cooked through and golden.

Serves 6

African Sosaties

This wonderful African style skewer of pork or lamb is marinated in a spicy apricot mixture before grilling.

1kg (2lb) boneless lean pork or lamb, cut into 2cm (³/₄in) cubes

Apricot Curry Marinade

220g (7oz) dried apricots

440ml (14fl oz) water

60ml (2fl oz) peanut oil

60g (2oz) butter

Pork and Stuffed Pepper Kebabs

African Sosaties, Moglai Kebabs

2 large onions, finely chopped

2 tblspn curry powder

60ml (2fl oz) red wine vinegar

1 red chilli, finely chopped

1¹/₂ tspn salt

1 To make marinade, place apricots and water in a saucepan over a medium heat and bring to the boil. Reduce heat and simmer until apricots are very soft. Remove from heat and set aside to cool slightly. Transfer apricots and liquid to a blender or food processor and process until smooth. Pour purée into a large bowl.

2 Heat oil and butter in a frying pan over a medium heat until butter melts, add onions and curry powder and cook, stirring, until onions are soft. Add onion mixture, vinegar, red chilli and salt to apricot mixture and mix to combine. Add meat cubes to mixture, cover and refrigerate overnight.

3 Drain meat, reserving marinade. Thread cubes onto pre-soaked wooden skewers and grill over medium coals, turning and basting occasionally with marinade, until meat is cooked through and crispy. Serve kebabs on a bed of rice with remaining marinade.

Serves 6

Moglai Kebabs

These beef or lamb kebabs are delicious with a rice pilau.

1kg (2lb) boneless lean beef or lamb, cut into small cubes

vegetable oil for basting

Yogurt Masala

1 onion, roughly chopped

2 cloves garlic

2.5cm (1in) piece fresh ginger, roughly chopped

200g (6¹/₂oz) natural yogurt

2 tspn ground coriander

1¹/₂ tspn ground turmeric

1¹/₂ tspn salt

1 tspn freshly ground black pepper

¹/₂-1 tspn chilli powder

¹/₂ tspn ground fenugreek

2 tblspn lemon juice

1 To make masala, place onion, garlic, ginger, yogurt, coriander, turmeric, salt, black pepper, chilli powder, fenugreek and lemon juice in a blender or food processor and process until smooth. Place meat cubes in a bowl, add masala and mix well to coat. Cover and set aside to marinate, stirring occasionally, for several hours at room temperature or overnight in the refrigerator.

2 Thread meat cubes, close together, onto pre-soaked wooden sticks or metal skewers and grill over hot coals, turning and basting frequently with oil, for 8-10 minutes or until tender.

Serves 6

Satay Ayam

Satays are quite different from the Middle Eastern kebabs, as the pieces of meat are cut much smaller, so they will absorb the seasonings properly.

2 large whole chicken breasts

1 large clove garlic, finely chopped

1/2 tspn salt

pinch ground white pepper

2 tblspn kechap manis or soy sauce

1 tblspn lemon juice

2 tblspn vegetable oil

Spiced Peanut Sauce, recipe follows

1 Remove skin from chicken, cut flesh from bones and cut into small cubes. Place garlic, salt and white pepper in a deep bowl and mix in kechap manis or soy sauce and lemon juice. Add chicken and toss until evenly coated. Cover and marinate for at least 30 minutes at room temperature or overnight in the refrigerator.

2 Thread chicken pieces onto pre-soaked bamboo skewers. Arrange on an oiled grill rack over moderately hot coals and cook, turning and brushing occasionally with oil, for 5 minutes or until chicken is tender and golden. Serve with Spiced Peanut Sauce.

Serves 8

Spiced Peanut Sauce

This sauce is delicious with chicken, beef, lamb or seafood satays. Serve the cooked skewers with steamed rice, prawn crackers (krupuk) and a few simple salads – a crunchy cucumber one or a tomato salad sprinkled with spring onions and fresh coriander.

60ml (2fl oz) vegetable oil

170g (5 1/2 oz) whole shelled peanuts or crunchy peanut butter

1 small onion, finely chopped

1 clove garlic, finely chopped

1 tspn dried shrimp paste

1/4 tspn chilli powder

salt

Satay Ayam, Spiced Peanut Sauce

1 tblspn peanut oil

315ml (10fl oz) water

1 tblspn instant tamarind or 1 tspn treacle blended with 3 tspn lemon juice

1 tspn brown sugar

1 If using whole peanuts, heat vegetable oil in a small saucepan over a medium heat, add peanuts and fry, shaking pan frequently, until peanuts are just brown. Remove nuts from pan and set aside to cool. Place peanuts in a blender or food processor, process to a coarse powder and transfer to a bowl.

2 Place onion, garlic and shrimp paste in blender or food processor and process to make a smooth paste. Add chilli powder and salt and briefly process to mix well.

3 Heat peanut oil in a saucepan over a medium heat, add the spice paste and fry gently, stirring, for a few seconds. Add water and bring to the boil, then add ground peanuts or peanut butter, tamarind or blended treacle mixture and sugar and mix to combine. Simmer, stirring frequently, until sauce thickens. Pour into a bowl and serve warm with assorted satays. (Sauce can be made well ahead and reheated gently.)

Steak Satay

1.5kg (3lb) sirloin or rump steak, cut into 2.5cm (1in) cubes

ground cumin seed

1 1/2 tspn lemon juice

Sesame Marinade

250ml (8fl oz) soy sauce

185ml (6fl oz) peanut oil

3 onions, finely chopped

2 cloves garlic, crushed

3 tblspn sesame seeds, toasted

1 To make marinade, place soy sauce, oil, onions, garlic and sesame seeds in a deep bowl and mix to combine. Add beef cubes, mix well to coat, cover and set aside to marinate for at least 3 hours.

2 Drain beef, reserving marinade. Thread steak onto small pre-soaked bamboo skewers and brush with a mixture of ground cumin seed and lemon juice. Cook over hot coals, turning and basting frequently with marinade, until tender.

Serves 8

Indonesian Prawn Satay

750g (1 1/2 lb) large uncooked prawns, peeled and deveined, leaving tails intact

vegetable oil

Chilli Lemon Marinade

125ml (4fl oz) coconut milk

3 tblspn lemon juice

1 tblspn soy sauce

1 tspn chilli paste

2 tspn grated lemon rind

2 cloves garlic, crushed with 1/2 tspn salt

1 To make marinade, place coconut milk in a large deep bowl, add lemon juice, soy sauce, chilli paste, lemon rind and garlic-salt mixture and mix to combine. Add prawns, turn to coat, cover and marinate 2-3 hours in the refrigerator.

2 Drain prawns, reserving marinade. Thread prawns onto pre-soaked bamboo skewers, 3-4 prawns per skewer. Brush with oil and cook on an oiled grill rack over hot coals for 2-3 minutes on each side, or until cooked through and golden.

3 Place reserved marinade in a small saucepan and bring to the boil over a medium heat. Reduce heat and simmer for 1 minute, adjust seasoning and serve with satays.

Serves 4

East Indian Satay

This thick marinade has a mildly spiced peanut flavour that is delicious with beef, pork or chicken.

1kg (2lb) boned chicken breast or thigh fillets or pork fillet, cut into 2cm (3/4in) cubes

Sweet Peanut Marinade

2 onions, chopped

2 cloves garlic

125ml (4fl oz) soy sauce

125ml (4fl oz) lemon juice

125g (4fl oz) peanut butter

45g (1 1/2oz) brown sugar

60ml (2fl oz) peanut or vegetable oil

1 tblspn ground coriander

dash Tabasco sauce

1 To make marinade, place onions, garlic, soy sauce, lemon juice, peanut butter, brown sugar, oil, coriander and Tabasco sauce to taste in a blender or food processor and process until smooth. Marinate cubed chicken or pork in this mixture for at least 2 hours.

2 Drain cubes, reserving marinade. Place 4 cubes onto each pre-soaked bamboo skewer. Cook on an oiled grill rack over moderately hot coals, basting occasionally with marinade, for 3-4 minutes on each side or until tender and golden.

3 Heat remaining marinade and serve with satays.

Serves 6

Chicken Livers En Brochette

Serve these flavoursome morsels on cocktail sticks with drinks, or grill on bamboo skewers and arrange on a bed of scrambled eggs for a late, leisurely breakfast.

500g (1lb) chicken livers, cleaned and trimmed

Sherry Mustard Marinade

250ml (8fl oz) medium dry sherry

125ml (4fl oz) olive oil

1 tblspn Dijon mustard

1 tblspn chopped fresh tarragon or 1 tspn dried tarragon

1 tspn salt

freshly ground black pepper

1 To make marinade, place sherry, oil, mustard, tarragon, salt and black pepper to taste in a bowl and mix to combine. Cut livers into halves or quarters, add to marinade and mix gently. Cover and marinate for 1 hour at room temperature or 3-4 hours in the refrigerator. Drain livers, reserving marinade.

2 Thread 2-3 pieces liver on each pre-soaked wooden cocktail stick, or 5-6 pieces on each bamboo skewer, pressing pieces tightly together. Brush with marinade and cook on an oiled grill rack over hot coals, brushing frequently with marinade, for 6-8 minutes until browned, but still pink in the centre. Serve immediately.

Serves 4-6

Yakitori

Sansho is available in powdered form from Japanese or oriental food stores. It has a fragrant peppery taste.

1kg (2lb) boneless chicken, cut into 3cm (1 1/2in) cubes

1 bunch spring onions, cut into 5cm (2in) lengths

2 green or red peppers, cut into 5cm (2in) squares

Soy and Sake Marinade

185ml (6fl oz) soy sauce

185ml (6fl oz) sake or mirin

60g (2oz) sugar

pinch powdered sansho or freshly ground black pepper

1 Thread chicken, spring onions and green or red peppers alternately on 8 pre-soaked bamboo skewers and arrange in a single layer in a shallow glass or ceramic dish. Place soy sauce, sake or mirin and sugar in a bowl and mix well to dissolve sugar. Pour mixture over the skewers, cover and set aside to marinate for 30 minutes, turning occasionally.

2 Drain skewers, reserving marinade in dish. Cook on an oiled grill rack over hot coals for 3 minutes, dip skewers into the marinade, turn and grill for 2 minutes more or until tender and glazed. Serve hot with a pinch of sansho or pepper.

Serves 4

Sesame Chicken Brochettes

6 boneless chicken breast fillets

60ml (2fl oz) light soy sauce

60ml (2fl oz) dry white wine or vermouth

1 tblspn sugar

1/4 tspn freshly ground black pepper

1 tspn grated fresh ginger

1 tblspn vegetable oil

100g (3 1/2oz) sesame seeds to coat

shredded spring onions for garnish

1 Cut chicken into bite-sized squares. Place soy sauce, wine or vermouth, sugar, black pepper, ginger and oil in a deep bowl and mix to combine. Add chicken and marinate for 20 minutes, turning occasionally.

2 Drain chicken, reserving marinade. Thread chicken onto 8 pre-soaked bamboo skewers, spacing squares a little apart so they will cook evenly.

3 Cook skewers on an oiled grill rack or hotplate, brushing several times with marinade, for 4 minutes on each side or until just tender. Remove from heat, brush with marinade and lightly roll skewers in sesame seeds to coat. Return to the barbecue for 1/2 minute each side or until seeds are toasted.

4 Arrange skewers on a heated serving platter, garnish with spring onions and serve immediately.

Serves 4

Yakitori, Sesame Chicken Brochettes

Scallops in Orange Ginger Sauce

750g (1¹/₂lb) scallops

Orange Ginger Marinade

125ml (4fl oz) freshly squeezed orange juice

2 tblspn teriyaki sauce

2 tspn bitters

2 tspn grated fresh ginger

freshly ground black pepper

1 Thread scallops evenly onto pre-soaked bamboo skewers. Lay flat in a shallow dish. To make marinade, place orange juice, teriyaki sauce, bitters, ginger and black pepper to taste in a bowl and mix well. Pour marinade over scallops, cover and refrigerate for 1 hour.

2 Drain skewers, reserving marinade. Cook on an oiled grill rack over moderately hot coals, brushing frequently with marinade, for 3-4 minutes on each side or until scallops are opaque. Serve immediately.

Serves 6

Brochettes Saint-Jacques

These skewers are delicious served with a sauce made from mayonnaise flavoured to taste with tomato purée.

8 large scallops, cut horizontally in half

16 large prawns, shelled and deveined, tails left intact

250ml (8fl oz) milk

¹/₄ tspn each, dried fennel, rosemary, summer savoury, basil and sage

seasoned flour

60ml (2fl oz) olive oil

1 tblspn butter

1 Thread scallops and prawns alternately onto 4 pre-soaked bamboo skewers, place in a shallow dish and pour milk over. Set aside to marinate, turning frequently, for 2-3 hours.

2 Drain and pat seafood dry with paper towels. Crumble dried herbs between fingers until very fine. Coat brochettes lightly with seasoned flour then sprinkle with herb mixture. Heat oil and butter together.

3 Cook brochettes on an oiled hotplate over moderately hot coals, turning occasionally and brushing with butter mixture, for 5-6 minutes or until prawns are tender and scallops are opaque. Serve immediately.

Serves 4

Prawns Teriyaki

Prawns grilled in the shell until they turn crunchy are wonderful eaten shell and all. Provide finger bowls and plenty of paper napkins.

750g (1¹/₂lb) uncooked prawns

Ginger Sherry Marinade

125ml (4fl oz) light soy sauce

60ml (2fl oz) peanut oil

2 cloves garlic, crushed

2 tblspn grated fresh ginger

small strip orange rind, finely shredded

2 tblspn dry sherry

2 tblspn brandy

1 Shell and devein prawns, leaving tail shells intact, or leave them in their shells, split each down the back and remove the vein. Place prawns in a deep bowl.

2 To make marinade, place soy sauce, oil, garlic, ginger, orange rind, sherry and brandy in a bowl, mix well and pour over prawns. Set aside to marinate for 2-3 hours, turning prawns occasionally.

3 Thread prawns onto pre-soaked bamboo skewers and cook over hot coals for 3-5 minutes or until they turn red and shells are opaque and crispy. Serve with remaining marinade for dipping.

Serves 4

Skewered Garlic Prawns

125ml (4fl oz) light soy sauce

125ml (4fl oz) vegetable oil

125ml (4fl oz) lemon juice

1 small onion, finely chopped

3 cloves garlic, chopped

1kg (2lb) uncooked prawns, shelled and deveined, tails left intact

6 spring onions, cut into 2.5cm (1in) lengths

fresh oregano or thyme sprigs

1 Place soy sauce, oil, lemon juice, onion and garlic in a large deep bowl and mix well. Add prawns, turning to coat in mixture, and marinate for at least 2 hours.

2 Drain prawns, reserving marinade. Thread onto pre-soaked bamboo skewers alternately with spring onions and little sprigs of herbs. Cook over hot coals, brushing often with marinade, for 5-6 minutes, depending on size of prawns, or until tender.

Serves 4

Prawns Teriyaki, Scallops in Orange Ginger Sauce, Brochettes Saint-Jacques

Shami Kebabs

These Indian minced meat kebabs are shaped the same but are seasoned quite differently from the kebabs of the Middle East.

60g (2oz) ghee or butter

1 large onion, finely chopped

3 cloves garlic, crushed

1kg (2lb) lean minced lamb or beef

1 tblspn ground coriander

1 tblspn plain flour

1 tblspn desiccated coconut

1 tblspn lemon juice

1 1/2 tspn salt

1 tspn ground ginger

1 tspn ground turmeric

1/2 tspn dried crushed red chillies

1/2 tspn freshly ground black pepper

1/4 tspn ground cinnamon

pinch ground cloves

vegetable oil for basting

1 Heat ghee or butter in a frying pan over a medium heat and cook onion and garlic, stirring, until onion is soft. Transfer mixture to a large bowl. Add mince to onion mixture with coriander, flour, coconut, lemon juice, salt, ginger, turmeric, red chillies, black pepper, cinnamon and cloves and mix with hands to thoroughly combine.

2 Divide mixture into 8 portions and mould each into a sausage shape around a flat metal skewer. Brush with oil and cook on an oiled grill rack over moderately hot coals, turning and brushing frequently with oil, for 8-10 minutes or until cooked through and brown. Serve with Indian breads and rice pilau.

Serves 8

Middle Eastern Kebabs

To serve these kebabs, place each inside a pocket bread and pull the skewer out. Serve with Tabbouleh (recipe page 46) or shredded lettuce.

500g (1lb) lean minced beef

1 small onion, grated

2 tblspn natural yogurt

1 tspn salt

2 cloves garlic, crushed

1 tblspn lemon juice

vegetable oil for basting

Baharat Spice Mixture

3 tblspn black peppercorns

1 1/2 tblspn coriander seeds

1 1/2 tblspn crumbled cinnamon stick

1 1/2 tblspn whole cloves

2 tblspn cumin seeds

1 tblspn cardamom seeds

3 tblspn ground paprika

1 tblspn ground nutmeg

1 To make spice mixture, place peppercorns, coriander, cinnamon, cloves, cumin and cardamom in a blender and blend to a coarse powder. Add paprika and nutmeg and briefly blend again. Store mixture in an airtight container.

2 To make kebabs, place mince, onion, yogurt, salt, garlic, lemon juice and 2 teaspoons of the spice mixture in a bowl and mix with hands to thoroughly combine. Divide mixture into 8 portions and mould each into a thin cigar shape around a flat metal skewer.

3 Brush kebabs with oil and cook on an oiled grill rack over moderately hot coals, turning and brushing with oil, for 6-8 minutes or until cooked through and brown.

Serves 4

Indian Kebabs in Pitta

500g (1lb) lean minced beef

1 small onion, grated

2 cloves garlic, crushed

1 tblspn plain flour

1 tblspn tomato purée

2 tblspn fresh lemon or lime juice

1/2 tspn ground cumin

1/2 tspn chilli

1/2 tspn coriander

pinch each, ground cinnamon, ginger, nutmeg and cloves

Tomato Sambal

2 tomatoes, diced

pinch each, ground cumin and coriander

salt

freshly ground black pepper

chopped fresh basil or coriander

To serve

6 small or 3 large pitta breads

vegetable oil or butter

6 lettuce leaves, shredded

cucumber slices

lemon slices

mint sprigs

1 To make sambal, place tomatoes in a bowl and season to taste with cumin, coriander, salt and black pepper. Add basil or coriander and toss lightly to combine. Set aside to allow flavours to develop.

2 Place mince, onion, garlic, flour, tomato purée, lemon or lime juice, spices and salt and black pepper to taste into a bowl and mix thoroughly with hands until combined. Divide mixture into 6 portions and mould each into a long, thin sausage shape around a flat metal skewer. Cover and chill, if possible, for 1 or 2 hours to firm.

Indian Kebabs in Pitta

3 Grill kebabs on an oiled grill rack over moderately hot coals, turning and basting occasionally with oil, for 10 minutes or until cooked through and well browned.

4 To serve, brush pittas lightly with oil or butter and grill lightly on both sides. Cut large pittas in half (if using). Open each pitta into a pocket and fill with shredded lettuce, Tomato Sambal and cucumber slices, then add a whole or half kebab. Garnish with lemon and mint.

Serves 6

Curried Kebabs

500g (1lb) lean minced beef
1 small onion, chopped
2 tblspn natural yogurt
1 1/2 tspn curry powder
1/2 tspn salt
1/2 tspn ground ginger
1/2 tspn garam masala
1/2 tspn grated lemon rind
1 tspn lemon juice
freshly ground black pepper
vegetable oil for basting

1 Place mince in a bowl, add onion, yogurt, curry powder, salt, ginger, garam masala, lemon rind, lemon juice and black pepper to taste and mix with hands to thoroughly combine. Divide mixture into 6 portions and mould each into a long cigar shape around a flat metal skewer.

2 Brush kebabs with oil and cook on an oiled grill rack over hot coals, turning and basting frequently with oil, for 6-10 minutes or until cooked through and brown.

Serves 3

A Touch of Spice

For many of us, our love affair with food prepared or cooked with spices begins at an Indian restaurant, but how often do we think of adding an Eastern influence when planning a barbecue? These recipes show how easy it is to adapt some of your favourite meals for outdoor cooking – they involve minimal preparation, use familiar cuts of meat and are sure to be a hit with the family.

Butterflied Lamb Indienne

A leg of lamb (boned, with the seam left open) is barbecued flat on the grill. In less than an hour it cooks to a rich brown outside with the thin portions well done and the thick portions slightly pink.

1 leg of lamb, butterflied
2 tspn ground coriander
1 tspn ground cardamom
1 tspn ground cumin
1/2 tspn ground turmeric
salt
freshly ground black pepper
100g (3 1/2 oz) natural yogurt

1 Lay the meat flat and slash through any thick portions not quite through and place in a large shallow dish. Rub lemon juice, spices, salt and black pepper to taste on all surfaces, then spread with yogurt and set aside to marinate for 1-2 hours, turning once or twice.

2 Lift meat from marinade and place flat, skin-side-down, on an oiled grill rack about 10cm (4in) above medium coals. Cook, turning and basting occasionally with marinade, for 1 hour or until cooked as desired. To carve, start at one end and slice across the grain.

Serves 6

Soy Ginger Chicken

2 x 1kg (2lb) chickens, split in 2
Soy Ginger Marinade
60ml (2fl oz) dry vermouth
60ml (2fl oz) soy sauce
1 tblspn soft brown sugar
2 tblspn grated fresh ginger
1/4 tspn freshly ground black pepper

1 To make marinade, place vermouth, soy sauce, sugar, ginger and black pepper in a deep bowl and mix to combine. Place chicken in marinade, turn to coat well and set aside to marinate, turning once or twice, for 1-2 hours.

2 Drain well, reserving marinade. Cook chicken over hot coals, turning and basting with marinade, for 20 minutes or until cooked and well glazed. Test by inserting a skewer into the thickest part of the flesh; juices should run clear.

Serves 4

Butterflied Lamb Indienne, Soy Ginger Chicken, Barbecued Bread (recipe page 42)

Hot Pepper Chops, Satay Lamb Chops

Satay Lamb Chops

6 lamb shoulder or leg chops

Satay Marinade

1 tblspn ground coriander

1 tspn ground cumin

1/2 tspn fennel seeds, crushed

2 small onions, quartered

2 cloves garlic

few strips lemon rind

1 tspn grated fresh ginger

1 tspn salt

1 tspn ground turmeric

2 tspn soft brown sugar

1 tblspn instant tamarind or 1 tspn treacle blended with 3 tspn lemon juice

60ml (2fl oz) water

4 tblspn vegetable oil

1 To make marinade, heat coriander, cumin and fennel seeds in a dry frying pan over a medium heat, stirring, until fragrant. Transfer to a large shallow glass or ceramic dish. Place onions, garlic, lemon rind and ginger in a blender or food processor and process to make a paste. Add to spice mixture in dish with the salt, turmeric, sugar and tamarind or blended treacle. Add water and mix well to combine.

2 Trim chops of skin and excess fat, add to marinade, turning to coat well. Cover and marinate for at least 2 hours at room temperature or overnight in the refrigerator.

3 Drain lamb, brush with oil and place on an oiled grill rack over medium coals. Cook, turning and basting occasionally with oil, for 8-10 minutes or until cooked as desired.

Serves 6

Hot Pepper Chops

6 lamb shoulder or leg chops

Chilli Garlic Marinade

2 tblspn vegetable oil

1 tblspn Worcestershire sauce

1 tblspn vinegar

1 clove garlic, finely chopped

1 fresh red chilli, finely chopped

1 tspn soft brown sugar

freshly ground black pepper

1 Trim chops of skin and excess fat and place in a shallow dish. To make marinade, place oil, Worcestershire sauce, vinegar, garlic, red chilli, sugar and black pepper to taste in a bowl and mix to combine. Pour over chops and set aside to marinate for at least 20 minutes, turning once.

2 Drain chops, reserving marinade. Cook lamb on an oiled grill rack over moderately hot coals for 2 minutes on each side. Lower heat or move chops to a cooler part of the barbecue and cook, turning and brushing with marinade, for 4-5 minutes more, or until cooked as desired.

Serves 6

Chilli Plum Pork Skewers

12 chicken livers, cleaned and trimmed

500g (1lb) pork fillet, in 1 piece

Chilli Plum Marinade

125ml (4fl oz) hoisin sauce

60ml (2fl oz) plum sauce

60ml (2fl oz) soy sauce

60ml (2fl oz) dry white wine

2 tblspn sugar

3 cloves garlic, crushed

1 fresh red chilli, sliced

1 tspn sesame oil

24 x 3cm (1¼in) pieces spring onion

1 To make marinade, place hoisin sauce, plum sauce, soy sauce, wine, sugar, garlic, red chilli and sesame oil in a medium bowl and mix well to combine. Pour half the marinade into a separate bowl.

2 Cut livers in half, place in a saucepan of boiling water and blanch for 1 minute. Drain well and place in one bowl of marinade, turning to coat. Cut fillet diagonally into 24 thick pieces then slit each piece almost through and butterfly out. Place in remaining marinade, mix well, cover and set aside to marinate for 30 minutes.

3 Drain pork and livers, reserving marinade. Wrap 1 chicken liver half and 1 piece spring onion in each slice of pork and thread 3 parcels loosely onto each of 8 pre-soaked bamboo skewers.

4 Cook skewers on an oiled grill rack over medium coals, turning and basting frequently with marinade, for 5 minutes on each side or until pork is tender and livers are just pink in the centre.

Serves 6

Chilli Plum Pork Skewers

Grilled Chicken Marylands

A chicken maryland is a leg and thigh quarter of the bird with the backbone removed. If unavailable, use a quartered chicken.

4 chicken marylands (leg and thigh joints)

4 bananas

red pepper rings and fresh coriander for garnish

Lemon Chilli Marinade

1 tblspn wine vinegar

1 tblspn lemon juice

1/2 tspn finely chopped fresh red chilli

2 cloves garlic, chopped

90ml (3fl oz) olive oil

1 To make marinade, place vinegar, lemon juice, red chilli and garlic in a bowl and whisk constantly, adding oil in a thin, steady stream, until mixture is thick. Place chicken in a large dish, coat with marinade, cover and set aside to marinate for 1 1/2-2 hours. Drain chicken, reserving marinade.

2 Place chicken and unpeeled bananas on an oiled grill rack over moderately hot coals and cook, basting occasionally with marinade, for 6-8 minutes on each side or until chicken is cooked through and golden. Transfer chicken to a heated serving platter and garnish with red pepper rings and coriander. Remove a thin strip of peel from each banana and serve with chicken.

Serves 4

Tandoori Chicken

To be authentic, Tandoori Chicken should be cooked in a clay oven called a tandoor, although this recipe adapts very well to the barbecue.

1.5kg (3lb) chicken, split in half

90g (3oz) ghee, melted

red onion rings, coriander sprigs and lemon wedges for garnish

Indian or Lebanese breads such as chapati, naan or pitta to serve

Tandoori Marinade

300g (10oz) natural yogurt

2 tspn ground turmeric

1 tspn ground paprika

1 tspn garam masala

1 tspn salt

1/2 tspn chilli powder

1/2 tspn ground cardamom

pinch powdered saffron

1 tblspn grated fresh ginger

1 tblspn lemon juice

1 To make marinade, place yogurt, turmeric, paprika, garam masala, salt, chilli powder, cardamom, saffron, ginger and lemon juice in a wide glass or ceramic dish and mix well to combine. Skin chicken, add to marinade and turn to coat thoroughly. Cover and chill for at least 6 hours, preferably overnight.

2 Remove chicken from marinade and place on an oiled grill rack over medium coals. Cook, turning frequently and basting with ghee, for 20-25 minutes or until tender and golden.

3 Garnish with onion rings, coriander sprigs and lemon wedges and serve with Indian or Lebanese breads.

Serves 4

Lebanese Poussin

Poussin, spatchcocks or chicken cooked this way are good served hot or cold with a salad.

4 tblspn lemon juice

2 tblspn olive oil

1/2 onion, grated

2 cloves garlic, crushed

1/2 tspn ground coriander

1/2 tspn salt

1 tblspn chopped fresh parsley

1 tblspn chopped fresh rosemary or 1 tspn dried rosemary

freshly ground black pepper

4 x 375-500g (12-16oz) poussin or spatchcocks, split in half

lemon wedges and shredded spring onions for garnish

1 To make marinade, place lemon juice, oil, onion, garlic, coriander, salt, parsley, rosemary and black pepper to taste in a wide, shallow glass dish. Add spatchcocks, turning to coat, cover and set aside to marinate for 1-3 hours at room temperature or overnight in the refrigerator.

2 Drain, reserving marinade. Place birds on an oiled grill rack over medium coals and cook, turning and basting occasionally with marinade, for 15-20 minutes or until juices run clear when thigh is pierced with a skewer. Serve garnished with lemon wedges and spring onions.

Serves 4

Tandoori Chicken

Chicken with Peach Salsa

Chicken with Peach Salsa

You can prepare the salsa well in advance and store in the refrigerator. Reheat to serve.

1 x 1.5kg (3lb) chicken, cut into serving pieces

Cumin Chilli Marinade

185ml (6fl oz) orange juice

60ml (2fl oz) olive oil

2 tspn ground cumin

1 tspn chilli powder

Peach Salsa

1 large fresh green chilli

1¹/₂ tspn chilli powder

125g (4oz) honey

125ml (4fl oz) chicken stock

2 peaches, peeled, stoned and diced

1 small clove garlic, crushed

1 To make marinade, place orange juice, oil, cumin and chilli powder in a large shallow dish and mix to combine. Add chicken pieces, turning to coat. Cover and set aside to marinate at least 1 hour at room temperature.

2 To make salsa, roast the green chilli over a gas flame or under a preheated hot grill until skin blackens. Using gloves, peel away the skin, cut off the top, discard seeds and finely chop. Place chilli in a small saucepan with chilli powder, honey, stock, peaches and garlic. Bring to simmering and simmer for 20 minutes or until mixture thickens slightly.

3 Drain chicken, reserving marinade. Place on a grill rack over medium coals and cook, turning frequently and basting with marinade, for 20 minutes or until tender. Serve with Peach Salsa.

Serves 4

Oriental Chicken Wings

1kg (2lb) chicken wings, wing tips removed

Five Spice Marinade

¹/₂ small onion, finely chopped

1 clove garlic, crushed

2 tblspn soy sauce

1 tblspn honey

1 tblspn tomato sauce

1 tblspn vegetable oil

pinch Chinese five spice powder

1 To make marinade, place onion, garlic, soy sauce, honey, tomato sauce, oil and five spice powder in a large bowl and mix to combine. Add wings, turning to coat, cover and marinate for several hours or overnight in the refrigerator.

2 Drain wings and cook on an oiled grill rack or barbecue hotplate, turning and basting frequently with marinade, for 10-15 minutes or until brown and crisp. Heat remaining marinade and serve with wings for dipping.

Serves 4

Pork Ribs with Plum Sauce

1kg (2lb) pork spareribs

Chinese Marinade

1 tblspn black beans

2 tblspn dry sherry

1 tblspn oyster sauce

1 tblspn light soy sauce

2 tspn Chinese five spice powder

freshly ground black pepper

Plum Sauce

1 tblspn peanut oil

1 large clove garlic, crushed

1 tspn grated fresh ginger

2 spring onions, finely chopped

170ml (5¹/₂fl oz) bottled plum sauce

90ml (3fl oz) chicken stock

1 tspn hot chilli sauce

1 tspn soy sauce

2 tspn cornflour blended with 1 tblspn cold water

1 To make marinade, place black beans in a bowl, cover with a little water and set aside to stand for 10 minutes. Drain beans and return to bowl, mash with a fork and stir in sherry, oyster and soy sauces, five spice powder and black pepper to taste. Trim excess fat from ribs. Coat ribs well with marinade and allow to stand for 10-15 minutes.

2 To make sauce, heat oil in a small saucepan over a medium heat, add garlic, ginger and spring onions and cook, stirring, until soft and fragrant. Add plum sauce, stock, chilli sauce and soy sauce to pan, heat to simmering and simmer gently for 5 minutes. Stir in blended cornflour mixture and cook, stirring, until sauce thickens and bubbles.

3 Drain ribs and discard marinade. Grill over moderately low coals for 5 minutes on each side. Brush with a little of the Plum Sauce and cook 5-10 minutes longer, turning once, or until ribs are tender and glazed. Cut ribs into small sections and serve with remaining Plum Sauce.

Serves 4

Pork Ribs with Plum Sauce

TWO BARBECUE MENUS

A special occasion, and where better to celebrate it than on your patio or balcony. These menus combine two traditional favourites – leg of lamb and grilled prawns – with unusual and delicious accompaniments that are sure to have your guests coming back for more.

SUMMER CELEBRATION

Serves 8

Bean and Potato Salad Tonnato

Barbecued Leg of Lamb

Roasted Red Peppers

Herb Sprig Salad

Hot Herb Bread

Summer Fruits Cheesecake

Bean and Potato Salad Tonnato

500g (1lb) green beans, trimmed

500g (1lb) butter or yellow wax beans, trimmed

1kg (2lb) baby new potatoes

chopped fresh parsley for garnish

Tuna Mayonnaise

200g (6¹/₂oz) canned tuna in oil

125ml (4fl oz) lemon juice

2 large egg yolks

4 garlic cloves, crushed

4 flat anchovy fillets

¹/₄ tspn cayenne pepper

¹/₂ tspn salt

125ml (4fl oz) vegetable oil

125ml (4fl oz) olive oil

1 Blanch beans in a large saucepan of boiling salted water for 5-8 minutes or until barely tender, drain and rinse under cold running water to stop the cooking process, drain and pat dry on paper towels. Cook potatoes in boiling salted water for 8-10 minutes or until just tender. Drain and halve or thickly slice.

2 To make mayonnaise, place undrained tuna in a blender or food processor, add lemon juice, egg yolks, garlic, anchovies, cayenne pepper and salt and blend or process until mixture is very smooth. With the machine running, add combined oils in a thin, steady stream and process until mixture thickens.

3 Arrange beans and potatoes on a serving platter. Spoon some of the tuna mayonnaise over vegetables, sprinkle with parsley and serve with remaining mayonnaise.

Serves 8

Roasted Red Peppers

4 cloves garlic, chopped

2 tspn oregano leaves

125ml (4fl oz) olive oil

4-6 red peppers, halved or quartered

chopped fresh parsley or coriander for garnish

1 Place garlic, oregano and oil in a bowl and set aside for 1-2 hours to develop flavour.

2 Place peppers on an oiled grill rack over moderately hot coals and cook, turning and brushing with flavoured oil, for 3-4 minutes on each side or until tender. Serve sprinkled with parsley or coriander.

Serves 8

Bean and Potato Salad Tonnato, Roasted Red Peppers, Herb Sprig Salad, Barbecued Leg of Lamb

Barbecued Leg of Lamb

1 large leg of lamb, butterflied

Mustard Mint Marinade

1 tblspn dry mustard

1 tspn crushed black peppercorns

2 tblspn lemon juice

2 tblspn olive oil

1 large bunch fresh mint

Butter Mint Sauce

90g (3oz) butter

1 onion, finely chopped

1 clove garlic, chopped

45g (1¹/₂oz) chopped fresh mint

1 To make marinade, place mustard, peppercorns, lemon juice and oil in a bowl and mix to combine. Rub the flattened meat thoroughly with marinade. Top with mint leaves, pressing them into meat, cover and set aside to marinate for at least 2 hours at room temperature.

2 To make sauce, melt half the butter in a saucepan over low heat, add onion and garlic and cook, stirring, for 5 minutes. Remove pan from heat and add remaining butter and mint.

3 Place lamb flat, mint-side-up, on a grill rack over moderately low coals, baste with warm mint sauce and cook for 20 minutes. Turn lamb, baste again and cook for 15-20 minutes longer for medium, 30-35 minutes for well done meat. Cut lamb into slices across the grain and serve with remaining sauce.

Serves 8

Herb Sprig Salad

assorted salad greens such as curly endive, witloof (chicory), small spinach leaves, watercress, mignonette and butter lettuce

fresh herb sprigs such as tarragon, green or purple basil, parsley

3 tblspn chopped fresh parsley

2 tblspn snipped fresh chives

Mustard Vinaigrette

1 tspn Dijon mustard

2 tblspn white or red wine vinegar

¹/₂ tspn salt

pinch sugar

freshly ground black pepper

6 tblspn olive oil

1 Wash salad greens and herb sprigs well and dry thoroughly in a salad dryer or in a clean tea-towel. Seal in a plastic bag and chill until crisp.

2 To make vinaigrette, whisk mustard with vinegar in a small bowl until combined. Add salt, sugar and black pepper to taste and whisk constantly, gradually adding oil, until dressing thickens.

3 To serve, tear salad greens and herbs into bite-size pieces and arrange in salad bowl. Pour over dressing, sprinkle with chives and parsley and toss well.

Serves 8

Hot Herb Bread

1 long loaf French bread

2 cloves garlic, crushed

¹/₄ tspn salt

2 tblspn chopped fresh mixed herbs

125g (4oz) butter, softened

1 Slash bread into 2.5cm (1in) slices almost through to the bottom crust. Crush garlic with salt then combine thoroughly with herbs and softened butter.

2 Spread butter on both sides of each slice of bread and over the top of loaf. Wrap bread in aluminium foil and heat over medium coals, turning frequently, for 15-20 minutes.

Serves 8

Summer Fruits Cheesecake

125g (4oz) crushed plain sweet biscuits

2 tblspn soft brown sugar

60g (2oz) butter, melted

Cheese Filling

315g (10oz) cream cheese, neufchatel cheese or cottage cheese

125g (4oz) caster sugar

2 eggs, separated

1¹/₂ tspn grated orange rind

3 tspn gelatine

3-4 tblspn freshly squeezed orange juice

2 tblspn freshly squeezed lemon juice

315ml (10¹/₂fl oz) double cream, whipped

Summer Fruit Topping

250-375g (8-12oz) prepared mixed fresh fruit such as whole blueberries, raspberries or strawberries; peeled sliced peaches, plums, mangoes; sliced kiwifruit, grapes

90ml (3fl oz) water

90ml (3fl oz) strained fresh orange juice or 2 tblspn lemon juice

2 tblspn sugar

2 tspn arrowroot blended with 1 tblspn cold water

1 To make base, place biscuit crumbs, brown sugar and butter in a bowl and mix until well combined. Press mixture in base of an oiled 20cm (8in) springform tin and chill until firm.

2 To make filling, beat cheese in a mixing bowl until light and fluffy. Gradually add caster sugar, then egg yolks and orange rind, beating until fluffy. Soak gelatine in orange juice in a small bowl over simmering water and stir until dissolved. Stir gelatine mixture and lemon juice into cheese mixture, then fold in whipped cream.

3 Beat egg whites to stiff peaks and lightly fold into cheese mixture. Pour mixture into prepared tin and chill until firm, several hours or overnight.

4 To make topping, wash and prepare fruit and set aside. Heat water, orange or lemon juice and sugar in a saucepan over a medium heat, stirring until sugar dissolves and mixture forms a light syrup. Stir in blended arrowroot and cook, stirring constantly, until thickened and bubbly. Remove from heat, stir in fruit and cool.

5 Remove cheesecake from tin and place on serving plate. Spoon fruit topping over and serve.

Serves 8

Summer Fruits Cheesecake

IMPROMPTU BARBECUE

Serves 6

Superb Guacamole

Charcoal Grilled Prawns

Grilled Tomatoes

*Anchovy Breadsticks
(recipe page 44)*

*Chick Peas in Wine
(recipe page 44)*

Mango Mousse

Superb Guacamole

1 large ripe tomato, peeled, seeded and chopped

3 spring onions, finely chopped

1 tblspn lemon or lime juice

1/2 tspn chilli powder

1/2 tspn ground coriander or 2 tspn chopped fresh coriander

2 tspn olive oil

freshly ground black pepper

1 ripe avocado, peeled, stoned and mashed

1 ripe avocado, peeled and cut into small chunks

Place tomato, spring onions, lemon or lime juice, chilli powder, coriander, oil and black pepper to taste in a bowl and mix to combine. Add mashed avocado and mix well, then lightly fold in avocado chunks. Adjust seasonings to taste and serve with corn chips, water biscuits or wedges of pitta or Lebanese bread.

Makes 600ml (1pt)

Charcoal Grilled Prawns

30-36 uncooked medium prawns

1 tblspn finely chopped fresh ginger

2 tblspn finely chopped fresh parsley

1 bay leaf

1/2 tspn chopped fresh thyme or 1/4 tspn dried thyme

1/4 tspn dried, crushed red chillies

salt

freshly ground black pepper

2 tblspn olive oil

2 tblspn fresh lemon juice

90g (3oz) butter

1 clove garlic, crushed

1 Using kitchen shears, cut along back rim of each prawn and rub gently under cold running water to remove black vein. Pat dry on paper towels. (You may peel the prawns or not, according to taste – they are best left on. If you peel them, leave tail segments intact.)

2 Place prawns in a large bowl, sprinkle with ginger, parsley, bay leaf, thyme, dried chillies, salt and black pepper to taste. Add oil and lemon juice, mix well and set aside to marinate at room temperature for 30 minutes.

3 Drain prawns and place on an oiled grill rack over moderately hot coals and cook for 2 minutes. Turn and cook 2-3 minutes longer or until prawns curl and turn pink. Melt butter with garlic in a small saucepan. When bubbling, discard the garlic, pour over prawns and serve immediately.

Serves 6

Grilled Tomatoes

A mixture of mature yellow tomatoes and red tomatoes will provide attractive colour.

6 firm-ripe tomatoes

4 tblspn olive oil

salt

freshly ground black pepper

2 tblspn finely chopped fresh basil

Neatly core tomatos and cut in half crosswise. Arrange halves, cut-side-up, on an oiled grill rack or hotplate over medium coals. Brush with oil and sprinkle with salt and black pepper to taste. Cook, turning once or twice, for 3-5 minutes or until heated through. Sprinkle with basil and serve immediately.

Serves 6

Mango Mousse

3 mangoes

75g (2 1/2oz) icing sugar, sifted

2 tblspn fresh lime or lemon juice

2 tspn gelatine soaked in 2 tblspn cold water

315ml (10fl oz) double cream, whipped

lime or lemon twists to decorate

1 Cut flesh from mangoes and place in a blender or food processor. Add icing sugar and lime or lemon juice and blend or process until smooth. Heat gelatine mixture in a small bowl over hot water until dissolved. Cool slightly, then stir into mango purée. Lightly fold in whipped cream.

2 Spoon mixture into individual glass bowls and chill until set. Decorate with lime or lemon twists before serving.

Serves 6

Charcoal Grilled Prawns, Grilled Tomatoes

BARBECUE EXTRAS

A great barbecue can't go without those extra special touches – a pre-meal nibble, a salad or two that co-ordinate with the grilled main course, appetising vegetable or bread accompaniments and a light, refreshing dessert. Look here for inspiration to help you make the menu complete.

Herb Loaf

1 round cottage loaf

4 tblspn chopped fresh parsley

2 tblspn chopped fresh mixed herbs

125g (4oz) butter, softened

1 tblspn lemon juice

2 tblspn grated mature Cheddar cheese

1 Cut loaf into 2cm (³/4in) thick slices, almost through to bottom crust. Place parsley, herbs, butter and lemon juice in a bowl and beat well until blended. Spread mixture between the slices.

2 Wrap loaf in heavy duty aluminium foil and place it over hot coals for 10-15 minutes. Open the foil and sprinkle loaf with cheese, then cook 10 minutes longer or until cheese melts.

Serves 8

Pilau Rice Salad

Spicy and dotted with fruits and nuts, good with barbecued lamb, kebabs or chops.

125ml (4fl oz) olive oil

410g (13oz) long-grain rice, rinsed and well drained

875ml (1¹/2pt) boiling water

75g (2¹/2oz) dried apricots, thinly sliced

2 slices fresh ginger, finely chopped

1 tspn ground coriander

1 tspn ground cumin

¹/2 tspn ground nutmeg

6 spring onions, finely chopped

90g (3oz) each, raisins and sultanas

60g (2oz) pine nuts, toasted

freshly ground black pepper

Fruit and Nut Garnish

12 dried apricots, poached in water for 3-4 minutes

toasted pine nuts

1 Heat 60ml (2fl oz) oil in a large saucepan over a medium heat, add rice and cook gently, stirring, for 5 minutes. Add boiling water and simmer gently, half-covered, for 15 minutes.

2 Add apricots to rice with ginger, coriander, cumin, nutmeg, spring onions, raisins, sultanas and pine nuts. Season to taste with salt and black pepper and lightly mix to combine. Cover and simmer 5 minutes longer or until rice is tender. Fluff rice with a fork and transfer to a serving platter. Drizzle with remaining oil and serve warm or at room temperature, garnished with apricots and nuts.

Serves 6

Barbecued Bread

This delicious bread is shown in the photograph on page 28.

large squares focaccia bread, cut into 3cm (1¹/4in) bars

garlic-flavoured olive oil

chopped fresh herbs, optional

Brush bread bars lightly with oil and sprinkle with fresh herbs (if using). Toast over medium coals, turning and brushing frequently with extra oil, until golden and crisp. Serve immediately.

Herb Loaf, Pilau Rice Salad, Tian Rouge (page 45)

Pommes Boulangeres

5 large potatoes

60g (2oz) butter

2-3 onions, thinly sliced

1 clove garlic, finely chopped

1 bay leaf

1 fresh thyme sprig or 1/8 tspn dried thyme

2 fresh parsley sprigs

315ml (10fl oz) chicken stock

salt

freshly ground black pepper

1 Peel and halve potatoes lengthwise, then cut crosswise into thin slices.

2 Melt butter in a large heavy saucepan or frying pan over a medium heat, add onions and garlic and cook, stirring, for 5 minutes or until onions are soft. Add potatoes, bay leaf, thyme, parsley and stock and season to taste with salt and black pepper.

3 Cover pan tightly and bring to the boil. Reduce heat and simmer for 10 minutes or until potatoes are almost tender. Uncover and briskly simmer for 10 minutes longer or until liquid reduces and potatoes are tender.

Serves 4

Anchovy Breadsticks

1 loaf unsliced sandwich bread

125g (4oz) unsalted butter

75g (2 1/2oz) canned anchovy fillets, undrained and mashed

1 tblspn lemon juice

freshly ground black pepper

1 Cut loaf lengthwise, not quite through bottom crust, into 2.5cm (1in) slices. Cut loaf crosswise into 2.5cm (1in) slices so you have equal-size sticks standing upright on the bottom crust. Place loaf on a double thickness of aluminium foil.

2 Melt butter in a small saucepan over low heat and stir in mashed anchovies, lemon juice and black pepper to taste. Brush sides and top of breadsticks with anchovy mixture, allowing it to drizzle down into the cuts. Wrap loaf in foil, sealing edges tightly.

3 Place on the barbecue over moderately-hot coals and heat, turning frequently, for 20 minutes. To serve, pull off breadsticks from bottom crust.

Makes about 40 breadsticks

Chick Peas or Corn in Wine

This dish from the South of France transforms canned chick peas or corn kernels into a lovely cold barbecue accompaniment.

90ml (3fl oz) olive oil

6 spring onions, finely chopped

2 cloves garlic, halved

2 x 315g (10oz) cans chick peas or sweet corn kernels, drained

125ml (4fl oz) dry white wine

1 tblspn chopped fresh thyme or 1 tspn dried thyme

2 tblspn lemon juice

2 small bay leaves

freshly ground black pepper

chopped fresh parsley or snipped chives for garnish

1 Heat oil in a large frying pan over a medium heat, add spring onions and garlic and cook, stirring, for 2-3 minutes or until onions are soft.

2 Add chick peas or corn to pan with wine, thyme, lemon juice, bay leaves and black pepper to taste. Heat to simmering and simmer for 10 minutes. Cool, then chill at least 3 hours before serving sprinkled with parsley or chives.

Serves 6

Vegetable Parcels

Wrap individual serves of prepared mixed vegetables loosely in double-thicknesses of aluminium foil, sealing the edges tightly. Cook on the barbecue about 10cm (4in) above moderately hot coals, turning occasionally. Parcels can also be cooked directly on the coals, but will need to be turned often. Allow a little less time than for cooking on the grill.

Potato Chive Cakes

500g (1lb) old potatoes

60g (2oz) butter

2 tblspn snipped fresh chives or chopped spring onions

salt

freshly ground black pepper

125g (4oz) plain flour

1 Peel potatoes and cook in boiling, salted water until tender. Drain and mash. Mix in butter and chives or spring onions while potatoes are still warm and season to taste with salt and black pepper. Gradually add flour, mixing to make a firm dough.

2 Divide dough in half. Pat each half out on a lightly floured surface to a circle about 5mm (1/4in) thick and cut into 4 triangles. Prick triangles all over with a fork.

3 Cook on an oiled hotplate over medium coals, turning once, until brown on both sides. Spread cakes with butter and serve immediately.

Serves 4.

Pommes Boulangeres, Potato Chive Cakes

Tian Rouge

3 red peppers, halved

4 tblspn chopped fresh Italian parsley

3 tblspn shredded fresh basil or
3 tspn dried basil

2 tblspn chopped fresh thyme or
2 tspn dried thyme

4 spring onions, finely chopped

90g (3oz) breadcrumbs, made from stale bread

6 large ripe tomatoes, peeled and cut into 2cm (³/4in) thick slices

olive oil

salt

freshly ground black pepper

1 tblspn capers

2 tblspn extra breadcrumbs

1 Brush peppers with oil and cook under a preheated hot grill until blackened and blistered all over. Place in a plastic food bag and set aside until cool enough to handle. Peel skin from peppers and discard. Cut peppers into 2cm (³/4in) wide strips.

2 Place parsley, herbs, spring onions and breadcrumbs in a bowl and mix to combine. Place one-third of the tomato slices in base of an oiled, shallow ovenproof dish and sprinkle with one-third of the herb mixture. Season to taste with salt and black pepper and drizzle with a little oil. Cover with half the pepper strips.

Repeat layers, then top with remaining tomatoes and herb mixture. Sprinkle top with capers and extra breadcrumbs and drizzle with oil.

3 Preheat oven to 180°C (350°F/Gas 4) and bake for 20-25 minutes or until bubbly and browned. Cool. Serve chilled or at room temperature.

Serves 6

Tabbouleh

This recipe is photographed on page 16.

125g (4oz) cracked wheat (burghul)

10 spring onions, finely chopped

60g (2oz) bunch flat-leaf parsley, chopped

6 tblspn chopped fresh mint

2 firm-ripe tomatoes, chopped

3 tblspn vegetable oil

60-125ml (2-4fl oz) lemon juice

salt

freshly ground black pepper

lettuce leaves to serve, optional

1 Soak wheat in cold water for 1 hour. Drain well and squeeze out excess liquid. Place wheat in a bowl, cover and refrigerate for 1 hour.

2 Add spring onions to wheat and mix well, crushing with the back of a spoon to slightly bruise the onions. Add parsley, mint, tomatoes, oil and lemon juice and mix thoroughly. Season to taste with salt and black pepper.

3 Line a salad bowl with lettuce leaves (if using) and spoon in the Tabbouleh.

Serves 6

New Potato Salad

10-12 small new potatoes

3 hard-boiled eggs, sliced

2 stalks celery, sliced

2 dill pickles, sliced

1 tblspn capers

2 tspn horseradish cream

125g (4oz) mayonnaise or sour cream

2 tblspn snipped fresh chives

Parsley Dressing

4 tblspn olive oil

2 tblspn vinegar

1 tblspn finely chopped onion

2 tblspn chopped fresh parsley

salt

freshly ground black pepper

1 Cook potatoes in boiling salted water for 8-10 minutes or until just tender. Peel (if liked) and, while still warm, cut into thick slices or quarters.

2 To make dressing, combine oil, vinegar, onion and parsley in a large mixing bowl and whisk until thickened. Season to taste with salt and black pepper, then add warm potatoes and toss lightly to coat. Set aside to stand until cool.

3 Add eggs, celery, pickles and capers to potatoes. Place horseradish cream and mayonnaise or sour cream in a small bowl, mix to combine and lightly fold through salad. Transfer to a serving bowl and sprinkle with chives.

Serves 6

Peach Cooler and Cream

4 ripe peaches, peeled, stoned and sliced

250ml (8fl oz) sweet white wine such as riesling, moselle or sauterne

2 tblspn brandy

1 tblspn fresh lime or lemon juice

caster sugar

grated fresh nutmeg for garnish

Whipped Cream Topping

315ml (10fl oz) double cream

2 tblspn icing sugar

1 tblspn fresh lime or lemon juice

1 Place peaches in a non-metallic bowl, add wine, brandy, lime or lemon juice and sugar to taste and lightly mix to dissolve sugar. Cover and refrigerate for at least 1 hour.

2 To make topping, beat cream with icing sugar until mixture begins to stiffen. Add lime or lemon juice and continue beating until stiff.

3 To serve, spoon peaches with liquid into serving glasses and top with dollops of cream. Garnish with nutmeg and serve, if liked, decorated with a mint leaf or tiny flower.

Serves 4

Pineapple Ice

This is refreshing on a hot, summery day, but the pineapple must be canned.

2 tspn gelatine

60ml (2fl oz) water

250g (8oz) sugar

1 litre (1³/4pt) water

250g (8oz) drained canned crushed pineapple

90ml (3fl oz) lemon juice

fresh mint sprigs for garnish

1 Set freezer at coldest setting. Soften gelatine in 60ml (2fl oz) water. Place sugar and 1 litre (1³/4pt) water in a saucepan over a medium heat and stir until sugar dissolves. Bring to the boil and boil, without stirring, for 5 minutes. Remove pan from heat, add gelatine mixture and stir until dissolved.

2 Transfer mixture to a bowl and chill for 45-60 minutes or until mixture begins to thicken. Stir in pineapple and lemon juice. Pour mixture into 1 deep or 2 shallow freezing trays and freeze until mushy.

3 Place mixture in a chilled bowl and beat with electric or rotary beater until smooth. Return to tray/s and freeze, stirring several times, until firm.

4 To serve, break up mixture with a fork and scoop into tall wine glasses or serving bowls. Garnish with mint.

Serves 6

Peach Cooler and Cream, Pineapple Ice

Index

Managing Editor: Rachel Blackmore
Editors: Liz Goodman, Linda Venturoni
Production Manager: Sheridan Carter
Senior Production Editor: Anna Maguire
Production Editor: Sheridan Packer
Editorial and Production Assistant: Danielle Thiris
Layout and Finished Art: Stephen Joseph
Styling Cover and Additional Internal Photography: Janet Mitchell

Published by J.B. Fairfax Press Pty Limited
80-82 McLachlan Avenue
Rushcutters Bay, NSW 2011
A.C.N. 003 738 430

Formatted by J.B. Fairfax Press Pty Limited
Printed by Toppan Printing Co, Hong Kong
PRINTED IN HONG KONG

© Margaret Fulton and Suzanne Gibbs (recipes)
© Ray Jarrett (photography)
© J.B. Fairfax Press Pty Limited (this edition), 1995
This book is copyright. No part may be reproduced or transmitted without the written permission of the publisher. Enquiries should be made in writing to the publisher.

JBFP 378 A/UK
Includes Index
ISBN 1 86343 116 0 (set)
ISBN 1 86343 211 6

Distribution and Sales Enquiries
Australia: J.B. Fairfax Press Pty Limited
Ph: (02) 361 6366 Fax: (02) 360 6262
United Kingdom: J.B. Fairfax Press Limited
Ph: (0933) 402330 Fax: (0933) 402234